怎麼增加人類全體的財富？
生命的意義與留給明天的財富

How to increase the wealth of all human beings?
The meaning of life and the wealth left to tomorrow

（中英雙語版）
(Chinese-English Bilingual Edition)

決長
Jue Chang

美商EHGBooks微出版公司
www.EHGBooks.com

EHG Books 公司出版
Amazon.com 總經銷
2022 年版權美國登記
未經授權不許翻印全文或部分
及翻譯為其他語言或文字
2022 年 EHGBooks 第一版

Copyright © 2022 by Jue Chang
Manufactured in United States
Permission required for reproduction,
or translation in whole or part.
Contact: info@EHGBooks.com

ISBN-13：978-1-64784-138-6

目錄

目錄 1

序 5

怎麼增加人類全體的財富？生命的意義與留給明天的財富。 7

    壹、前言。 7
    貳、錢與生命的意義的關係。 7
    參、人類為什麼要工作？ 9
    肆、怎麼增加人類全體的財富？ 10
    伍、比較與應用。 12
        一、慾望。 12
        二、利與義。 13
        三、未來的藍圖。 14
        四、科學會帶來毀滅？ 14
        五、玩耍與環保。 15
        六、政府預算。 16
        七、競爭。 16
        八、聯合國的援助。 17
    陸、結語。 18

明天是未知的嗎？生命的意義與明天的特性。 20

    壹、前言。 20
    貳、舊觀念和舊觀念的缺點。 21
    參、有不變的事物。 24
    肆、明天的特性。 26
    伍、比較與應用。 27

陸、結語。..29

轉型正義與生命的意義 30

壹、前言。..30
貳、正義與生命的意義的關係。..........................31
參、轉型正義的核心問題。................................32
肆、威權是舊的正義。......................................33
伍、忠誠的缺點。...35
陸、自由與自由的缺點。...................................36
柒、尋找新價值。...37
捌、筆者的答案。...39
玖、台灣人的反應。...41
拾、結語。..44

Preface 46

How to increase the wealth of all human beings? The meaning of life and the wealth left to tomorrow. 48

Section 1 : Introduction 48
Section 2 : The relationship between money and the meaning of life.49
Section 3 : Why do humans have to work?...........................51
Section 4 : How to increase the wealth of all human beings?........52
Section 5 : Comparison and Application..............................55
  1. Desire. 56
  2. Profit and Justice. 57
  3. The blueprint for the future. 58
  4. Science will bring destruction? 58
  5. Play and environmental protection. 59

6. Government budget. 60

7. Competition. 61

8. The assistance of the United Nations. 62

Section 6：Conclusion. 64

Is tomorrow unknown? The meaning of life and the characteristics of tomorrow. 65

Section 1：Preface. 65

Section 2：The old ideas and the shortcomings of the old ideas. 66

Section 3：There are constant things. 70

Section 4：The characteristics of tomorrow. 73

Section 5：Comparison and Application. 74

Section 6：Conclusion. 76

Transitional Justice and the Meaning of Life 78

Section 1：Preface. 78

Section 2：The relationship between justice and the meaning of life. 79

Section 3：The core issue of transitional justice. 80

Section 4：Authoritarianism is the old justice. 82

Section 5：The Shortcomings of Loyalty. 84

Section 6：Freedom and the shortcomings of freedom. 85

Section 7：Search for new value. 87

Section 8：The author's answer. 89

Section 9：The reaction of Taiwanese. 92

Section 10：Conclusion. 96

怎麼增加人類全體的財富？生命的意義與留給明天的財富。

序

　　筆者的故鄉是台灣，台灣的政治人物常常大喊：「我們要愛台灣。」「捍衛台灣價值。」

　　這是一件奇怪的事，台灣的學者們說：生命的意義是無解的難題，沒有任何人可以定義別人的人生。

　　真是矛盾，沒有任何人可以定義別人的人生，但是我們必須要愛台灣，我的人生被定義了。

　　大學的教授說：明天是未知的，父母不應該定義子女的人生。但教授們教育學生要遵守道德，學生們的人生被定義了。

　　台灣以前是威權的，台灣現在反對威權，台灣反對標準答案，政治人物和大學教授都反對「標準答案」。

　　筆者發現了這個矛盾，生命的意義是人類歷史中最難的題目，所有的哲學家都沒有答案。而筆者發現了生命有意義。

　　筆者發現了：「生命有意義，人有義務維護環境、人有義務為自己負責。」

　　學校應該告訴學生：「你要為自己負責，人有義務維護自己的心靈，人有義務豐富心靈。」

　　政治人物應該告訴人們：台灣以前沒有標準答案，但現在有答案了，台灣要更富足、更進步、更深耕文化，台灣已經找到未來的方向了。

　　「先是珍惜生命，然後豐富心靈、累積財富。」這是一件簡單的事，但怎麼證明呢？於是筆者寫了三篇論文來說明與證明，分別是：

「怎麼增加人類全體的財富？生命的意義與留給明天的財富。」

「明天是未知的嗎？生命的意義與明天的特性。」

「轉型正義與生命的意義。」

　　筆者想要告訴人們生命有意義，但筆者受到嘲笑了，「太好笑了，有一個瘋子說他解答了生命的意義。」期刊也不認為簡單的發現是論文，但生命的意義依然是重要的題目，筆者還是該將這三篇論文公開發表，於是有了本書。

2021、11、16　決長

怎麼增加人類全體的財富？生命的意義與留給明天的財富。

壹、前言。

美國有一個美國夢，美國希望每一個人都富有，中國有一個中國夢，中國希望每一個人都富有，每一個國家都有政治人物說一樣的話吧！「我要讓每一個人都富有。」這是容易受到民眾歡迎的話，因為「每一個人都富有」是人類長久以來的夢想。

當然，政治人物只是隨口說說，「每一個人都富有」這不可能吧！如果每一個人都富有了，那麼誰來清理水溝呢？「每一個人都富有」這真的是不可能的事嗎？有的，還是有方法可以增加人類全體的財富。本篇論文將說明：「怎麼增加人類全體的財富？」

本篇論文將說明：

一、錢與生命的意義的關係。

二、人類為什麼要工作？

三、怎麼增加人類全體的財富？

四、比較與應用。

本篇論文將說明：

依照大自然的特性，人類有必須要做的工作。

這同時也是「人活著要做什麼？」的答案。

生命不是虛無，有人類應該追求的財富。

貳、錢與生命的意義的關係。

「怎麼增加人類全體的財富？」在筆者回答這個問題之前，筆者要先說明錢是什麼，筆者要先說明：「生命的意義與錢的關係。」

錢是什麼呢？為什麼這張紙可以買東西？為什麼這張紙可以換到財貨與勞務？當我拿出鈔票，店員就允許我拿走他的商品，當我拿出鈔票，店員就願意為我提供服務，只是一張紙，為什麼紙可以換到麵包呢？錢和其他的紙不一樣，錢的上面有國王（政府）的印章，基於國王（政府）的擔保，所以錢有價值，錢是有公信力的紙，錢的價值來自於公信力，國家是錢的依靠。

國家是錢的依靠。錢很重要，國家很重要，如果沒有國家、沒有銀行、沒有法律、沒有警察，你的財產將不再是你的財產，你的財產會被強盜拿走，人民無法安穩地生活。

「錢很重要，國家很重要。」這件事人類已經知道了嗎？

「生命有意義，人有義務維護環境，人有義務維護社會。」這件事人類已經知道了嗎？

生命的意義是人類歷史上最難的題目，哲學家說：生命的意義沒有答案，人類沒有必須要做的事。耶穌和佛陀說：錢不重要，天堂比較重要。人類很矛盾，「國家很重要，我們必須要維護我們的家園，但生命沒有意義，人類沒有必須要做的事。」筆者發現了這個矛盾，筆者發現了：「生命有意義，我們必須要維護我們的家園，這是活著應該要做的事。」

人與人合作，然後才有國家，國家的背後也有一個依靠，守法的人比不守法的人多，喜愛和平的人比喜愛戰爭的人多，正常的人比瘋狂的人多，有求生意志的人比沒求生意志的人多，當多數人願意維護我們的家園，國家才能存在。「人類願意求生存，人與人互相合作，才有國家，才有錢。」

參、人類為什麼要工作？

先是生存，先是求生意志，人類互相合作，然後才有國家，然後才有錢。

本篇論文的題目是：「怎麼增加人類全體的財富？」

在筆者回答這個問題之前，在這一小節筆者要先說明：「人類為什麼要工作？」

生命的意義是人類歷史上最難的題目，

「人活著要做什麼？」沒有哲學家可以回答這個問題。而筆者發現了：「生命有意義，人類有必須要做的工作。」

生命的意義這個題目是怎麼來的呢？

因為地球上有人類，人類活在地球上，所以人類被迫要面對今天，人類被迫要面對「今天要做什麼？活著要做什麼？」

然後有了生命的意義這題目。

錢也是一樣的，「人類為什麼要工作？」

因為人有身體、因為人會餓，所以人類必須工作。

生命有意義，因為人有身體、因為人會餓，所以人類必須工作。

同樣的，因為人類擁有地球，所以人類必須維護地球。

我有我的家，我要整理我的房間，

我有我的故鄉，我的故鄉需要有人掃落葉、清水溝。

我擁有一個和平有法律的故鄉，我要付稅金給警察。

因為人類有身體，所以人類要運動。

因為我有家人,所以我要保持聯絡。

因為我擁有今天,所以我必須安排今天,

因為我有心靈,所以我必須管理我的心靈,我需要娛樂,我需要愛。

「怎麼增加人類全體的財富?」

這題目的答案不會像政治人物吹牛的那麼美好,地球的資源就那麼多,人類一直都會餓,人類要一直為了吃飯而工作,社會運轉著,我們要一直維護社會機制,就算放長假了,我也需要安排我的假期,就算待在房間裡,我也需要管理我的心靈。

生命有意義,因為人類擁有身體、擁有地球、擁有心靈,所以人類必須要工作。

肆、怎麼增加人類全體的財富?

人類為了飢餓工作,為了維護社會機制、維護環境、維護心靈而工作。

吃飯、消化、吃飯、消化,佛陀說食物終究是虛無,

吃飯、消化、吃飯、消化,筆者的故鄉有許多水果,有時候會因為水果太多而丟棄水果。「怎麼增加人類全體的財富?」答案不是更多水果、更多工廠。因為飢餓是固定的,所以答案不是:「砍伐森林、種植更多農田、蓋更多工廠。」

怎麼增加人類全體的財富?

答案不是印更多鈔票,答案不是砍伐森林,種植更多農田。

怎麼增加人類全體的財富?

這題目是「生命的意義」,

人類活著要追求什麼？

什麼是人類的財富？

吃飯、消化、吃飯、消化，一餐又一餐，一餐又一餐，在消化之後，人類有得到什麼嗎？我們可以留下什麼給一千年以後的人類嗎？

有的，吃飯、消化、吃飯、消化，吃飯不是一成不變的，我們和一千年以前的人不一樣，我們有冰淇淋，這是一個偉大的發明，這是我們的財富。

一千年前的人類常常散步，到處走走，我們也常常散步，到處走走，但是我們有汽車，這是我們的財富。我們有紅綠燈，我們有交通規則，交通規則保護我們的安全，這是我們的財富。

一千年前的人類只知道要從河裡抓更多的魚，而我們知道我們應該要維護我們的家園，我們有法律、我們培養了公德心，我們有維護環境的觀念與習慣，這是我們的財富。

從前，農民被大地主欺壓，農民再怎麼努力都不會變富有，而現在筆者的家鄉，勞工可以組成工會，勞工可以上街遊行，這是我們的財富。

從前，人民只知道要聽國王的話，國王常常像強盜一樣拿走人民的財富，而現在我們知道我們有義務監督政府，在筆者的家鄉，政府會發放津貼給老人與殘障人士，「我們有義務監督政府」這個觀念是我們的財富。

從前，人類常常戰爭，現在人類知道戰爭很可怕，人類知道核子武器很可怕，對戰爭的恐懼是我們的財富，「我們知道我們有義務維護和平」這個觀念是我們的財富。

從前，人類不知道活著要做什麼，因為無聊與茫然很多人選擇了尋求刺激，很多人選擇了惹事生非，很多人選擇了欺負弱小，筆者發現了：生命有意義，人有義務維護自己的心靈。筆者的發現是人類的財富。現在有漫畫，有許多比賽，有許多歡笑與流汗的方法，這是人類的財富。

從前，人類害怕著世界末日，人類不知道要為永續做準備。從前，生命的意義沒有答案，人類害怕思考生命的意義。政治人物高喊著愛國、高喊著價值，卻從來沒有人回答為什麼要愛國。筆者發現生命有意義：「人類有義務維護環境、人類有義務為自己負責。」財富有一個基礎，愛自己的人比不愛自己的人多，關心社會的人比不關心社會的人多，關心環境的人比不關心環境的人多，有求生意志的人比沒求生意志的人多，這是人類的財富。

每一個人都富有，這就是文明進步了，可以化為文字的科學進步了，不能化為文字的愛與求生意志增加了。

伍、比較與應用。

筆者發現了：「先是生存，先是求生意志，然後是和平與合作，然後才是財富。」

筆者發現了：「世上的資源有限，人類的飢餓也是固定的，怎麼增加人類的財富呢？答案是豐富心靈、文化進步。」

這是一個簡單的發現，而這是新的發現嗎？而這是重要的發現嗎？在這一個小節，筆者將說明筆者的發現會帶來什麼改變，這個小節是比較與應用。

一、慾望。

「世上的資源有限，人類的慾望無窮。」為了滿足人類無窮的慾望，所以你應該學會理財，所以你應該讀經濟學。這是經濟學的前言。

「因為慾望,所以你應該賺錢。」

這是錯誤的,慾望是可有可無的,慾望不是信念,慾望也不是人類前進的動力。

「因為慾望,所以你應該賺錢。」

這樣的觀念無法回答:「怎麼增加人類的財富?」

如果慾望是財富的原動力,當人類要增加財富,當人要增加原動力,人類必須增加慾望更加貪婪?

而筆者的答案是:依照大自然的特性,

人類有義務維護環境,有義務維護自己的心靈,有義務堅定求生信念,求生信念是人類的財富。

二、利與義。

「為了滿足人類無窮的慾望,所以你應該學會理財。」慾望是一個負面的字眼,利益與正義常常出現衝突。

耶穌說:富有的人很難進天國。

佛陀說:錢財是遮蔽心靈的灰塵。

學校的老師說:追求利益的是小人,追求道德的是君子、是紳士。

富有是人類的夢想,但是生命的意義沒有答案,「人應該追求富有嗎?」這問題沒有答案,人類不確定是否應該追求富有,

人類很矛盾、人類很無奈,「人類不確定是不是應該追求富有,但我們不是聖人,我們有慾望,所以我們追求財富。」以前人們的觀念是這樣的。

在政治上，支持民主、支持人權的人們也犯了一樣的錯誤，「民主價值」、「普世價值」，支持民主的人們大聲地喊著民主價值，美國政府喊著普世價值，價值是主觀的，人們分不清楚民主是主觀的還是客觀的，支持民主的人們說：「民主雖然不能當飯吃，但民主很重要。」

而筆者提出了：「科學可以當飯吃，民主可以當飯吃。」

「民主可以當飯吃，民主真實地影響我們的生活，這不是理所當然的嗎？」也許有讀者會這樣誤會。不，這不是理所當然的，以前民主是主義與價值，美國政府大喊：普世價值。以前人們分不清楚主觀與客觀，「民主是客觀的。」這個觀念是筆者提出的。

三、未來的藍圖。

「為了滿足慾望，所以你應該要賺錢。」慾望沒有指出未來的藍圖。

生命的意義是一個難題，人類沒有未來的藍圖。國家的預算要花在哪裡？我們要怎麼建設我們的國家？我們要走向怎樣的未來？這些問題沒有答案，於是人們只知道要蓋更多的工廠、蓋更高的大樓。

而筆者提出：「接下來的一萬年，人類活著要做什麼？這問題的答案是永續。」

我們要建設一個溫暖而永續的家園。

四、科學會帶來毀滅？

科學對人類是好的嗎？科學能帶來幸福嗎？科學會不會帶來毀滅？人類對科學一直有這樣的疑慮，當天文學發展的時候，教會迫害了科學家，當人類要登陸月球時，許多人感到害怕，擔心踏上月球會觸怒上帝。人類對大自然感到害怕，人類也對科學感到害怕。

在恐懼中，科學還是進步了，但是人類認為生命沒意義，沒有未來的方向，人類踩著凌亂的步伐，做了傷害環境的事，做了傷害彼此的事，當人類嚐到苦果時，人類說：科學會害人、知識會害人，財富也會害人墮落。

而筆者提出：地球的資源是大致固定的，一天又一天、一餐又一餐，人類可以累積什麼財富嗎？

有的，人類可以更加認識大自然，人類可以更加認識人類，學會和大自然相處，學會和彼此相處，豐富的心靈，對大自然的認識，這是人類的財富。

五、玩耍與環保。

在舊觀念中，追求道德是崇高的，追求利益是低俗的，道德與利益相衝突。同樣的，重視環保的人是崇高的，重視利益的人是低俗的，環保與利益是衝突的。同樣的，心靈與物質常常衝突、愛情與麵包常常衝突、玩耍與認真讀書常常衝突，特別是在孔子的教育中，讀書才能對社會有貢獻，玩耍是荒廢生命。

面對這些的衝突，雖然有人說我們應該要兼顧，但利與義的衝突並沒有被解開，環保與利益的衝突繼續著，玩耍與認真讀書的衝突繼續著。

而筆者提出了：

「維護環境不是因為主觀的價值，維護心靈不是因為主觀的價值。這是客觀的事實，人類擁有地球、人類擁有心靈，人類有義務維護地球、有義務維護心靈，這是人類的工作。」

六、政府預算。

筆者的故鄉是台灣，和世界上其他政府一樣，每隔幾年我們的政府就會制定一個大計畫，然後國會通過許多預算，政治人物會蓋很多東西，蓋了很多東西之後，政治人物就可以炫耀：「看啊！我的政績真是豐碩。」

爭取更多預算、蓋更多東西，追求「偉大」，然後炫耀，這是政治人物的習慣。

可是不追求「偉大」嗎？政府的預算要怎麼花呢？不追求「偉大」又該追求什麼呢？

接下來的一萬年，人類要追求什麼呢？

關於未來，我們要追求什麼？

生命是題目，生命是答案，人類應該追求的就是「日常」。

不要面子工程，人民要的就是基礎建設，

少蓋一點工程也沒關係，國家追求的不是偉大，國家追求的是正常與健康。

七、競爭。

人類應該彼此競爭嗎？

這也是一個難題。

有人認為：人類應該競爭，如果努力的人和不努力的人拿到一樣多的錢，這是不公平的，競爭幫助人類進步，所以我們應該支持資本主義。

有人認為：人類不應該競爭，應該讓所有人都吃到一樣的麵包。

而且現在科技變發達了，富豪有機器的幫助，沒有機器、沒有資本的人一定會輸，汗水換不到麵包，窮人會越來越窮，所有我們應該反對資本主義。

在過去，生命的意義沒有答案，「人類應該怎麼活？」這問題沒有答案，「人類是不是應該競爭？」這問題沒有答案。

而筆者發現了生命有意義。

人類有義務維護自己的胃，人類也有義務維護社會。

吃是人類永遠的追求，和平也是人類永遠的追求。

當和平降臨了之後，人類依然要每天吃飯，餐廳每天都要端出料理，好吃與難吃就形成了競爭，人類每天都要吃飯，餐廳的競爭會永遠持續下去，各行各業的競爭會永遠持續下去。但這是競爭，這不是戰爭，當人們在競爭時，人民也有義務提醒國家，人民要叫國家去照顧跌倒的人。

八、聯合國的援助。

當聯合國在幫助落後國家時，

聯合國也遇到了相似的問題：

「怎麼讓整個國家變富有？」

他們會提供金錢援助、物資援助，聯合國知道：給人魚不如教人釣魚。聯合國也會提供教育援助，蓋學校、教導學生一技之長。聯合國也會蓋廁所與淨水設備和太陽能發電設備⋯⋯

這樣就能讓一個國家變富有了嗎？

還有其他的問題。

先進國家無法幫助不肯為自己而努力的國家。

落後國家的獨裁者揮霍無度，但人民卻依然冷漠，人民沒有反抗，人民不在乎自己的稅金被浪費掉，大部分的援助都被獨裁者拿走了，國家的財富無法累積，人民冷漠、國家貧窮。

但怎麼叫人民不要冷漠呢？

美國試著輸出民主，

美國說：民主很珍貴。

但美國沒有說：生命有意義，生命很珍貴。

面對恐怖主義時美國依然雞同鴨講，

恐怖分子認為：生命的意義是為了神轟轟烈烈地犧牲。生命的意義是報復世界的不公平。生命的意義是刻下深深的傷痛。

但哲學家依然說：生命的意義是無解的難題。

美國說：民主很珍貴。

美國沒有說：生命有意義，生命很珍貴。

陸、結語。

生命不是虛無，人類生存在地球上。

人類被迫面對今天，人類被迫面對飢餓，人類必須滿足飢餓，人類必須填入今天，人類必須滿足心靈，這是強迫接受的祝福，人類必須要追求富足。

生命不是虛無，人類生存在地球上。

人類面對著地球，人類有義務維護地球，

地球是人類唯一的家。

怎麼增加人類全體的財富？

我們可以為我們的家園增加什麼財富？

我們可以增加公德心，我們可以建立法律制度，我們可以建立維護環境的習慣，我們可以建立關心社會的習慣，我們可以發展科學，我們可以更加認識大自然，人類可以永遠追求下一餐，人類可以永遠追求和平，人類可以追求音樂與歡笑。

生命有意義，接下來的一萬年，人類應該豐富心靈，人類應該建立一個溫暖的文明。

明天是未知的嗎?生命的意義與明天的特性。

壹、前言。

在畢業典禮時,大學校長常常會告訴畢業生:「你們要離開校園了,你們會面對未知的未來,會有未知的挑戰,老師們沒有關於未來的答案,你們要自己找答案。」

這是一個未解的難題,

明天是未知的,未來是沒有答案的。

和生命的意義一樣,

「明天要做什麼?」

「接下來的人生要做什麼?」

「人活著要做什麼?」

這個問題沒有答案,

「明天」和「生命的意義」都最難的題目。

明天是未知的嗎?

本篇文章將說明題目與答案,

本篇文章將先說明「人們對明天的恐懼與矛盾」然後再說明答案,

本篇論文將說明:

一、舊觀念和舊觀念的缺點。

二、有不變的事物。

三、明天的特性。

四、比較與應用。

本篇論文將說明：生命有意義，明天有特性，有一個光明的未來，那是人類的方向。

貳、舊觀念和舊觀念的缺點。

在過去的觀念中：明天是未知的。

科學家認為：未來是難以預測的。

耶穌說：末日的審判會突然地降臨。

佛陀說：你不一定可以看到明天的太陽。

科學與宗教都說：明天是未知的。

也許今天是平常的一天，一樣和家人吃早餐，吃完早餐後一樣地去上班、上學，但意外隨時都可能突然到來，你深愛的一切可能會突然消失。

明天是未知的，這就代表今天的美好隨時可能會消失，「明天是未知的」這想法連帶影響著今天。

今天的努力是對的嗎？今天的努力是值得的嗎？努力在公司做好一個職位，希望能讓家人過好日子，和家人累積美好的回憶，為了這小小的幸福而努力是對的嗎？這小小的幸福是真正有價值的嗎？

不一定，明天是未知的，今天覺得珍貴的事物，也許明天又變了。

佛陀說：家人的愛是短暫的。

耶穌說：只有上帝的愛是永恆的。

在未知的未來的面前，今天的美好都像泡沫一樣脆弱，凡夫的努力都是沒有用的。

知識也是一樣，人類的知識在神的面前都是廉價的，今天的知識到了明天也許是錯的，凡夫不可能觸及真理。

因為明天是未知的，所以你不能確定你今天的知識是對的。

因為明天是未知的，所以你不能確定你今天所做的一切是不是值得的。

因為明天是未知的，所以今天的善與惡是不確定的。

因為明天是未知的，所以今天的一切都是不確定的，人們沒有一項肯定的知識。

「明天是未知的」這個觀念帶來了不確定，也帶來了恐懼。

「明天是未知的」這問題帶來了另一個問題：「愛會消失，對不對？」

愛不是永恆的吧！

沒有永恆的愛吧！

山盟海誓常常是假的，

今天緊緊抱著的人，隨著時間進行，懷中的溫暖很脆弱，懷中的溫暖很快就會消失了，財富不是永恆的，美食總是一下子就消化掉了，甚至健康與有形的一切都一樣脆弱。

「愛」真的值得人去愛嗎？

「愛」禁得起時間的考驗嗎？

「愛」是對的嗎？

也許我們應該看輕平庸的愛，

也許我們應該去尋求上帝永恆的愛。

明天是不確定的，

愛也是不確定的，

於是人類常常感到疑惑與恐懼。

「未知」帶來了負面的影響。

「明天是未知的」這個觀念帶來了不確定，也帶來了茫然。

「明天是未知的」這問題帶來了另一個問題：「生命沒意義。」

　　明天是未知的，今天覺得有價值的事物，也許到了明天就變得沒有價值了，沒有真正有價值的事物，人類也沒辦法為明天留下財富。

　　人活著該追求什麼呢？哲學家的答案是「不知道。」

　　該追求利益嗎？但是錢買不到天國的門票，錢不是永恆，名聲、地位、財富是脆弱的，意外與死亡隨時會降臨，人總有死亡的一天。

　　錢也不等於幸福，就算握住幸福了，幸福也很快隨著時間從手中流失了，追求利益是沒有意義的。

　　該追求與利益無關的快樂嗎？堆骨牌、玩遊戲、看漫畫、下棋、畫畫、唱歌、放煙火……

　　一樣的，快樂不是永恆，快樂只是快樂，快樂的時光總是過得很快，煙火消失後沒有留下什麼。

　　不管人們做什麼都是沒有意義的。

因為「明天是未知的」，

所以「人類應該為明天做什麼？

應該為明天留下什麼？」

這個問題沒有答案。

因為「明天是未知的」，

所以「人類應該走向怎樣的未來？」

這個問題沒有答案。

於是人類茫然地活著，一下子追求利益，一下子追求與利益無關的快樂，

但又矛盾地說：「追求利益是沒有意義的。」

但又矛盾地說：「追求快樂是沒有意義的。」

明天是未知的，「活著要做什麼？」這問題沒有答案，人們沒有未來的方向，人們活在茫然之中。

參、有不變的事物。

明天是一個難題，

「人類活著要做什麼？」

是一個難題，

生命的意義是人類歷史上最難的題目。

人類不知道活著要做什麼，

人們對明天保持著恐懼。

而在這個小節中，筆者將說明：「明天有特性，有不變的事物。」

明天是未知的，人類沒有找到永恆，人類沒有找到未來不會改變的事物。

這是舊的觀念。

那大自然中有沒有不變的事物呢？

有的，人類已經找到了，

但是人類不知道：「已經找到了。」

人們依然無法戰勝恐懼，

人們依然困惑。

這是一件矛盾而令人混淆的事。

明天是未知的，

一個實驗了一萬次的物理定律，如果明天要做第一萬零一次，會得到相同的結果嗎？

不知道，又還沒有做，結果是不確定的，這是科學的極限，科學家無法預測未來。

一個實驗了一萬次的物理定律，如果明天要做第一萬零一次，會得到相同的結果嗎？

知道且確定，如果條件不變，結果肯定會相同，物理定律是不會改變的。

科學家有沒有發現不會改變的事物呢？

有的，科學就是去認識大自然，然後從中找出規律。大自然有規律，科學家也發現了許多具有重現性的法則。

地球繞著太陽運轉，大自然有規律性，

把東西拿起來再放手，牛頓發現了：「地球有吸引物體的力量」，這是一項可以一再重現的大自然的特性。

阿基米德在兩千年前發現了浮力原理，你也可以去洗澡，你也可以去實驗，浮力原理是一項可以一再重現的大自然的特性。

人類有沒有發現不會改變的事物呢？

好像有，又好像沒有，

人類不知道：「已經找到了。」

人類無法戰勝對明天的恐懼。

而筆者發現了人類的這個矛盾，

筆者發現了明天有法則，

「明天有確定的法則，生命確定有意義。」這是筆者的發現。

肆、明天的特性。

明天有什麼特性呢？

有沒有什麼事在一萬年以後還是對的？

有的，太陽還有幾十億年的壽命。一萬年以後，太陽依然會在那裡。

地球已經存在幾十億年了，在人類滅亡之前，地球會一直在那裡。

如果準備維護環境的對照組和不維護環境的實驗組，我們會發現人們有義務維護環境，「人們有義務維護環境」這在一萬年以後還是對的。

如果準備清醒的志願者和喝醉的志願者,然後讓他們玩賽車比賽,或是改成生活中的其他情境,我們會發現人們必須注意自己的安全,「人們有義務照顧自己」這在一萬年以後還是對的。

如果人類停止維持社會機能,社會機能將會停止,「人們有義務維護社會」這在一萬年以後還是對的。

如果人類停止維持和平,人類將會失去和平,「人類有義務維護和平」這在一萬年以後還是對的。

「生物都會新陳代謝,人類有吃飯的需求,如果人類生存著,人類需要吃飯。」這在一萬年以後還是對的。

「人類有思考的能力,人類有心靈,人類有情感上的需求,如果人類生存著,人類必須要照顧心靈,人類必須要去愛,人類必須要一直一直去愛。」這在一萬年以後還是對的。

這些都是明天的特性,

這些都是「人類活著要做什麼?」的答案。

伍、比較與應用。

筆者發現了:「太陽一直都在,明天也要好好吃飯。」

筆者發現了:「生命有意義,明天有該做的事。」

這是一個簡單的發現,而這是新的發現嗎?而這是重要的發現嗎?在這一個小節,筆者將說明筆者的發現會帶來什麼改變,這個小節是比較與應用。

一、當青少年問:「生命的意義是什麼?」,過去哲學家回答不知道,以後學校的老師不應該再回答不知道,學校應該告訴學生:生命真的有意義。

二、過去人類活在恐懼之中，人類害怕黑夜、害怕閃電、害怕大自然，也害怕明天。而筆者發現了：「太陽一直都在，明天也要好好吃飯。」明天有一個明確的方向，接下來的一萬年，人類要繼續維護地球。

三、人類有義務維護社會、有義務維護環境，人類有義務為自己負責。學校應該告訴學生：「你有義務。」學校不應該說：「不知道、不確定。」

四、明天是未知的，人類的知識總是有些不確定，宗教家總是說：「在神的面前，人類一無所知。」而筆者找到了確定的事：「接下來的一萬年，人類要繼續愛地球。」不需要依靠神，筆者發現了確定的事。

五、愛會消失，佛陀說吃飯不重要，佛陀說家人的愛像泡沫一樣脆弱，耶穌說只有上帝的愛是永恆的。佛陀錯了，佛陀只有看到飯會消化、會消失。佛陀不知道：「只要人還活著，人要一直吃飯。」

佛陀不知道：「只要人類還存活在地球上，人類要一直去愛。」

六、民主與獨裁那個比較好，這題目一直沒有答案，人又不是神，關於未來，誰可以說他是對的呢？國王與菁英不一定是對的，可是多數也不一定是對的。

因為未來是未知的，對與錯是不確定的，民主與獨裁那個比較好是不確定的。

而筆者發現：「生命有意義，人民有義務關心社會。」

獨裁國家不允許人民關心社會，所以獨裁錯了。

筆者的發現是真實而確定的，

民主與獨裁不再是無止盡的爭論。

七、明天是未知的，人類的知識總是有些不確定，而筆者發現：「明天有特性，有確定的事。」有了確定的根基之後，人們可以在這根基之上再累積，大自然有許多具有重現性的事，人類可以更加詳細地描述大自然的特性，有了確定的根基之後，人類可以累積更多確定的智慧。

陸、結語。

筆者發現了：「明天有特性。」

筆者發現了：「大自然有特性，生命有特性，人類有義務維護環境、有義務關心社會、有義務思考、有義務為自己負責。」

筆者的發現是件簡單的發現，但這是一個重要的發現。

也許有讀者會誤會，也許有讀者會以為這是一件人類早就知道的事，筆者再強調一次，生命的意義是人類史上最難的題目，挑戰這題目的所有哲學家都失敗了，以前人類活在疑惑與恐懼之中，人類擔心著隨時會降臨的世界末日，人類歌頌著愛卻又不確定愛是不是真的值得去愛。

「明天有特性，生命有意義。」

這是筆者的發現。

轉型正義與生命的意義

壹、前言。

筆者的故鄉是台灣，台灣以前是威權的，

台灣現在走在民主的道路上，台灣人民已經可以投票選總統了，台灣人有信仰的自由。當我們在介紹民主時，我們會提到信仰的自由。

這是一個矛盾，曾經，信仰民主的人和信仰威權的人發生了激烈的衝突，

當我們在介紹民主時，我們不應該說：「信仰是自由的。」我們應該要說明那段衝突的歷史，我們應該要說明：「為什麼我們不可以信仰威權？」

轉型正義就是「正義」改變了，

文化與信仰改變了，

「我們應該怎麼活？」這題目有新的答案了。

本篇論文將說明：

一、正義與生命的意義的關係。

二、威權是過去的正義。

三、自由與尋找新的答案。

四、新的答案。

轉型正義就是正義的改變，

本篇論文將說明「我們應該怎麼活？」

本篇論文將說明：

「為什麼舊的觀念是錯誤的？

新的答案是什麼？」

貳、正義與生命的意義的關係。

人類出現在地球上，於是人類被迫要面對「今天」，人類被迫面對「人應該怎麼活著？」這個問題，這就是生命的意義這個題目的由來，而哲學家們給出的回答是：不知道。

同樣的，地球上不是只有你一個人，地球上有很多人，人類要面對其他人，「人應該怎麼活著？」這個題目就變成了「我們應該怎麼活著？」而這就是「正義」。

「我們應該怎麼活？」

有沒有共同的答案？

有沒有普世價值？

什麼是對？什麼是錯？

什麼是善良？什麼是邪惡？

有沒有什麼法則，

那個法則是所有人都應該遵守的？

符合那個法則的就是正義，

違反那個法則的就是錯誤。

有沒有什麼方向，

那個方向是我們國家追求的？

符合那個方向的就是正義,

違反那個方向的就是錯誤。

「正義」存在嗎?

就是「共同的法則」存在嗎?

有沒有什麼法則是所有人類都應該遵守的?

參、轉型正義的核心問題。

台灣在中國的東南方,在二次世界大戰之後,蔣介石敗給了共產黨,蔣介石從中國帶了兩百萬人來台灣,蔣介石在台灣實施威權統治。

蔣介石的支持者認為:蔣介石是二次世界大戰的英雄,蔣介石帶領著國家走過艱難的時刻,蔣介石的支持者為蔣介石立了很多銅像,銅像的下方寫著:「民族英雄。」

蔣介石是正義的英雄,蔣介石就是台灣的正義。

而爭取自由的人們認為:蔣介石是實施威權統治的獨裁者,在獨裁之下,蔣介石殺了很多台灣人,蔣介石是殺人魔王。

爭取自由的人說:「威權是不好的,獨裁者是邪惡的,蔣介石是邪惡的,銅像是威權象徵。」

但為什麼呢?

為什麼威權是錯的?

為什麼民主是對的?

因為支持自由的人們拿到政權了,所以民主就是對的?

支持自由的人們一直沒有給出說明。

為什麼蔣介石是邪惡的？

你們是神嗎？你們憑什麼審判人？

蔣介石以前是二次世界大戰的英雄，

為什麼現在變成了大壞蛋？

審判的依據是什麼？

「以前是邪惡，現在是正義，是嗎？為什麼？」

這是轉型正義中的第一個問題。

台灣的執政黨現在正在拆除銅像，

原本放蔣介石銅像的地方現在要放什麼？什麼是新的正義？（什麼是台灣價值？）

這是轉型正義中的第二個問題。

「為什麼舊時代是錯的？」和「新的觀念是什麼？」

這是轉型正義中的兩大問題。

很多支持自由的人並沒有思考這問題，

而是直接認為銅像是威權象徵，銅像都是邪惡的。

「為什麼舊時代是錯的？」和「新的觀念是什麼？」這是轉型正義的核心問題。

肆、威權是舊的正義。

為什麼舊時代是錯的？在筆者回答這個問題之前，

筆者要先說明舊時代的答案是什麼。

台灣曾經發生過一場大地震，台灣人在災區立了紀念碑，

紀念碑提醒下一代：不要忘記大自然的力量。

這就是銅像的本質，銅像和紀念碑一樣都是叮嚀。

「人生中最重要的事是什麼呢？」

「人應該怎麼活著呢？」

銅像就是這問題的答案。

圖書館的書太多了，

如果我們只能告訴下一代一句話，

我們要留下什麼呢？銅像就代表了那句話，

銅像是文化的總結，銅像就是生命的意義的答案。

巴西里約立了巨大的基督像，

這就表示巴西告訴著下一代：

「人應該怎麼活著呢？人要聽神的話，

生命中最重要的事是什麼呢？生命中最重要的事是聽神的話，生命的意義是神。」

孔子的門徒立了孔子的銅像，這就表示：

「人應該怎麼活著呢？臣下要有臣下的樣子，兒子要有兒子的樣子，生命的意義是禮。」

有人立了原住民英雄的銅像，這就表示：

「不要忘記反抗，不要忘記祖靈。」

怎麼增加人類全體的財富？生命的意義與留給明天的財富。

有人立了救難英雄的銅像，這就表示：

「生命的意義是捨己救人。」

有人立了傳奇運動員的銅像，這就表示：

「生命的意義是永不放棄。」

而國家領導人的銅像就代表著：

「生命的意義是忠誠。」

這就是道德與正義，所有人都應該忠誠，忠誠是所有人都應該遵守的法則，

忠誠是舊時代的善。

伍、忠誠的缺點。

什麼是善？我們應該怎麼活著？

我們應該遵守什麼？

過去的答案就是「忠誠」。

以前的人們不知道什麼是善？

當社會出現衝突時，誰該聽誰的話呢？

直覺而缺乏理由地，子女應該聽父母的話，人民應該聽國王的話，因為國王是國王，所以我們應該聽國王的話。因為國王是國王，然後才有了法律與秩序，然後國家才得以維持，人民才能被法律保護，如果將軍們失去了忠誠，那就會是一連串的戰爭。

「基於上帝與國王的旨意，人們應該守法。」忠誠這個觀念是法律的根基，忠誠就是善，忠誠是「人應該怎麼活著？」的答案。

但國王等於法律是危險的，因為國王在維持秩序的同時，國王才是最放縱的人，甚至國王是滿手鮮血的人。

蔣介石也是類似的，

蔣介石的支持者認為蔣介石保護了國家、安定了國家，但蔣介石是滿手鮮血的人。

陸、自由與自由的缺點。

國王等於法律是危險的，於是有人起身反抗國王，同時也挑戰舊觀念，人不應該忠誠，人應該自由，國家的未來不應該由國王決定，國家的未來應該由多數決定，權力太集中不好，權力應該分散，

善是什麼呢？善沒有標準答案。

善沒有標準答案，支持自由的人沒有回答善是什麼，自由的理由只是反抗。

主張自由的人說：「我主張自由。」

主張忠誠的人說：「我主張忠誠。」

你有你的主張，我有我的主張，

雙方爭吵著。

支持自由的人說：「自由是普世價值。」

支持忠誠的人說：「忠誠才是普世價值。」

支持自由的人說：「自由是美好的。」

支持忠誠的人說：「自由會亂。」

支持自由的人說：「國家的未來應該由人民決定。」

支持忠誠的人說：「多數就是對的嗎？我們是平凡人，聽國王的話比較好。」

支持自由的人說：「獨裁者雙手染滿了鮮血。」

支持忠誠的人說：「國王有功有過，你們不要妄下定論，你們憑什麼審判人，你們就是對的嗎？支持忠誠是我的自由，你們憑什麼管我？」

支持忠誠的人說：「忠誠是善。」

支持自由的人說：「善沒有標準答案。」

善沒有標準答案，那為什麼支持忠誠的人要聽支持自由的人的話呢？於是轉型正義陷入了長久的爭吵。

柒、尋找新價值。

自由是反威權，支持自由的人認為自由是新的價值，但又覺得疑惑，自由只是反威權，我們還沒有新的價值，台灣需要新的價值。台灣正在拆除蔣介石的銅像，那原本放銅像的地方要放什麼呢？新的價值是什麼呢？台灣價值是什麼呢？於是台灣人努力找尋新的價值。

台灣有一座聖山，那座聖山為台灣阻擋了颱風的災害，玉山強壯又偉大，台灣價值是玉山精神。

台灣人普遍是熱情的，台灣價值就是人情味。

台灣人的祖先和水牛有很深的感情，水牛耕耘著，水牛不怕吃苦，台灣價值就是水牛精神。

台灣有一個菜販，她的學歷不高，她默默地持續捐錢，數十年，持續地幫助弱勢團體，這是台灣價值。

台灣有一個棒球投手，他當上洋基隊的王牌投手，腳踏實地，一球一球投，這是台灣價值。

　　台灣有一位反抗殖民統治的英雄，這是台灣價值。

　　台灣有一位為了爭取自由而自焚的烈士，這是台灣價值。

　　台灣的信仰中有一位保護漁民的女神，這是台灣價值。

　　中國很可惡，堅決反對九二共識，這是台灣價值。

　　台灣的蔡英文總統說：「台灣共識就是經由民主的程序來凝聚共識。」

　　台灣價值就是我們要找出台灣價值，

　　你說一件偉大的事，我說一件偉大的事，

　　每個人都說一件偉大的事，然後我們一起討論，這樣就可以找到台灣價值了吧！

　　你說一件偉大的事，我說一件偉大的事，

　　台灣人尋找台灣價值的方法和人類尋找生命的意義的方法是一樣的。

　　有人說生命的意義是為社會服務，

　　有人說生命的意義是犧牲，

　　有人說生命的意義是幽默，

　　有人說生命的意義是音樂，

　　有人說生命的意義是保護家人，

　　有人說生命的意義是尋找心中的寧靜，

怎麼增加人類全體的財富？生命的意義與留給明天的財富。

有人說生命的意義是像小狗一樣玩耍,

有人說生命的意義是挑戰極限,

有人說生命的意義是學吃苦,

有人說生命的意義是閱讀,

有人說生命的意義是回天堂,

有人說生命的意義是出人頭地,

有人說生命的意義是交到知心好友,

有人說生命的意義是品嚐好咖啡⋯⋯

有好多的答案,但為什麼是那個答案呢?

理由呢?真的嗎?

台灣價值和生命的意義有很多答案,

但每一個答案都沒有理由。

捌、筆者的答案。

生命有沒有意義?我們應該怎麼活?有沒有什麼法則是全人類都該遵守的?

生命的意義曾經是人類歷史上最難的題目,但是筆者已經找到答案了。

筆者發現大自然有法則,基於大自然的法則,生命有意義,生命的意義是「自決、多元、共好、永續。」

人類活著要做什麼?接下來的一萬年,人類活著要做什麼?想著接下來的一萬年,答案就是「永續」。這是可以用實驗證明的答案,只要準備維護環境的實驗組和不維護環境的對照組，我們可以發現大自然有法則，我們可以發現人類有義務維護環境，這是人類活著該做的事，生命的意義是「永續」。

人類活著要做什麼？我這一輩子要做什麼？這就是一件該做的事，我要回答我的人生，答案是「自決」。這是可以用實驗證明的答案，只要讓清醒的志願者和酒醉的志願者玩賽車遊戲，就可以證明酒醉的危險，也可以證明人要注意自己的安全。大自然有這樣的法則：人有義務照顧自己，人要對自己的人生負責，生命的意義是「自決」。

人類活著要做什麼？今天我們要做什麼？

我們要對我們的今天負責，答案是「共好」。這是可以用實驗證明的答案，只要停水、停電，就可以證明我們有義務維護社會機制。

大自然有這樣的法則：我們有義務維護社會，生命的意義是「共好」。

人活著要做什麼？今天我要做什麼？

太陽就在那裡，今天就在那裡，

這是真實的，有一個空白的今天等我填入，自由發揮就代表著創造力，我必須回答今天，人有義務思考，我必須豐富我的心靈。

這是真實的，空白的今天就在眼前，生命的意義是「多元」。

不是沒有答案而多元，而是依照大自然的法則，每一個人都有義務思考，有一個答案是「多元」。這是一個所有人都應該遵守的法則。

人與人是不同的嗎？

人與人有相同點，

每一個人都應該照顧環境，

每一個人都應該維護社會，

每一個人都應該關心國家，

每一個人都應該為自己負責。

人與人之間有相同點也有不同點，這也是一個相同點，每一個人都應該學習尊重。

依照大自然的特性，生命的意義是：「自決、多元、共好、永續。」

筆者發現了：大自然有法則。

筆者找到了共同的法則，

「我們應該怎麼活？」這問題有共通的答案。

為什麼獨裁是錯的？因為人有義務關心社會，而獨裁國家禁止人民關心國家。所以獨裁是錯的。

「為什麼舊時代是錯的？」和「新的觀念是什麼？」筆者已經回答了這兩個問題。

玖、台灣人的反應。

有一個轉型正義中常出現的矛盾，

支持自由的人說：自由是人的天性，台灣人喜愛自由，台灣人從很久以前就在追求自由，台灣人一直都喜愛自由。

這是一個矛盾：「過去是黑暗的時代，但台灣人一直都喜愛自由。」

「自由是受歡迎的，但先烈們受盡迫害。」支持自由的人在歌頌自由的時候，常常把自由說成了童話，真正的轉型正義應該是:「以前是黑暗的時代,人們不喜愛自由,人們喜愛忠誠,現在我們認為是先烈的人,他們以前是大眾眼中的反賊。」

轉型正義是從不懂到懂的過程,

新的觀念不是一開始就受歡迎。

新的觀念不是一開始就受歡迎,

筆者找到答案了:

「依照大自然的法則,人有義務思考、有義務為自己負責、有義務關心社會、有義務維護環境,生命的意義是自決、多元、共好、永續。這就是台灣未來的方向。」

而當筆者告訴台灣人:「生命有意義」的時候,台灣人並沒有感到開心,

筆者得到少許的鼓勵和許多的嘲笑。

「哇!有一個瘋子說他找到生命的意義的答案了。」

「笑死人了,生命的意義不會有答案啦。」

台灣嘲笑著筆者的答案,

然後台灣出現了很多「本來」,

人「本來」就應該思考,

人「本來」就不應該冷漠,

人民「本來」就有義務監督國家,

台灣「本來」就是命運共同體。

台灣還出現了很多奇怪的「多元」，

因為生命的意義沒有答案，所有我們要多元。

因為台灣有高山、大海、森林、草原，台灣物種豐富，所以台灣價值是多元。

因為台灣有原住民、有漢人、有來自菲律賓、越南、印尼的人，所以台灣價值是多元。

因為科技發達了，台灣蓬勃發展，所以台灣價值是多元。

因為台灣學習了中國文化、日本文化、歐洲文化，還有自己的本土文化，所以台灣價值是多元。

因為神創造了多彩的世界，所以耶穌支持多元，因為耶穌支持多元，所以台灣價值是多元。

因為佛陀沒有我執，所以我們要學習尊重，所以台灣價值是多元。

因為台灣人熱情、包容，所以台灣價值是多元。

「笑死人了，生命的意義不會有答案啦。」

但台灣價值突然有答案了，

蔡英文總統說：「台灣價值是共好。」

然後蔡總統底下的部長、市長、媒體、學者紛紛表示共好就是最好的答案了，

然後就出現了很多奇怪的「共好」。

政治人物說：「我從政以來都是為大眾謀福利，共好一直是我的

政治哲學,台灣價值是共好。」

因為共好一直都是台灣人長久的願望,所以台灣價值是共好。

因為台灣是我們的母親,所以台灣價值是共好。

因為先烈犧牲、反抗,因為先烈勇敢不自私,所以台灣價值是共好。

因為人權是普世價值,所以台灣價值是共好。

因為台灣人熱情好客,所以台灣價值是共好。

因為我們應該愛台灣,所以台灣價值是共好。

新的答案是怎麼來的呢?

沒有理由,沒有出處,卻有答案,

這是一件奇怪的事。

拾、結語。

轉型正義就是「正義」和人們尋找答案的過程、

人們接受答案的過程。

正義存在嗎?

有共通的法則嗎?

「為什麼舊的觀念是錯誤的?

新的答案是什麼?」

有摸索答案的過程嗎?

有接受答案的過程嗎?

轉型正義就是深耕文化，從不懂到懂的完整過程才是轉型正義。

以前的正義是忠誠，後來人們爭取自由，

因為忠誠不好，人們尋找新的答案。

以前生命沒意義，人沒有必須要做的事。

而現在有新的答案了，

筆者發現了：生命有意義，每一個人都應該思考，

每一個人都應該關心社會。

本篇論文回答了：

「為什麼舊的觀念是錯誤的？

新的答案是什麼？」

筆者已經找到了共通的法則，

「我們應該怎麼活？」

這個問題有共通的答案。

Preface

The author's hometown is Taiwan,

and Taiwan's politicians often shout:

"We must love Taiwan."

"To defend Taiwan's values."

This is a strange thing.

Scholars in Taiwan say: The meaning of life is an unsolvable problem. No one can define other people's lives.

It is a contradiction. No one can define other people's lives, but we must love Taiwan. My life is defined.

University professors said: tomorrow is unknown, parents should not define the life of their children. But professors educate students to abide by ethics, and their lives are defined.

Taiwan used to be authoritarian, Taiwan now opposes authoritarianism, Taiwan opposes the standard answer, and politicians and university professors oppose the "standard answer."

The author found this contradiction. The meaning of life is the most difficult topic in human history. All philosophers have no answer. And the author has found that life has meaning.

The author found out: "Life is meaningful, people have an obligation to maintain the environment, and people have an obligation to be responsible for themselves."

Schools should tell students: "You have to be responsible for yourself. People have an obligation to maintain their own minds , and people have an obligation to enrich their own minds."

Politicians should tell people: There was no standard answer in Taiwan before, but now there is an answer. Taiwan's direction is to become more prosperous, more progressive, and more deeply cultivated in its culture. Taiwan has found its future direction.

"First cherish life, then enrich the mind and accumulate wealth." This is a simple matter, but how to prove it? So the author wrote three papers to illustrate and prove, namely:

"How to increase the wealth of all mankind? The meaning of life and the wealth left for tomorrow."

"Is tomorrow unknown? The meaning of life and the characteristics of tomorrow."

"Transitional justice and the meaning of life."

The author wanted to tell people that life is meaningful, but the author was mocked. "It's so funny, there is a madman who said he answered the meaning of life."

And journals don't consider simple discoveries to be papers.

But the meaning of life is still an important topic.

The author should publish these three papers publicly,

So there is this book.

2021、11、16　*Jue Chang*

How to increase the wealth of all human beings? The meaning of life and the wealth left to tomorrow.

Section 1 : Introduction .

The United States has an American dream. The United States wants everyone to be rich. China has a Chinese dream. China wants everyone to be rich. Every country has politicians who say the same words! "I want to make everyone rich." This is a word that is easily welcomed by the people, because "everyone is rich" is a long-term dream of mankind.

Of course, politicians just said casually,

"Everyone is rich" This is impossible! If everyone is rich, who will clean the gutter? Is "everyone rich" really impossible? Yes, there are still ways to increase the wealth of all mankind. This paper will explain: "How to increase the wealth of all human beings?"

This paper will explain:

1. The relationship between money and the meaning of life.

2. Why do humans have to work?

3. How to increase the wealth of all human beings?

4. Comparison and Application.

This paper will explain:

According to the characteristics of nature, human beings have work that must be done.

This is also the answer to "What should people live to do?"

Life is not emptiness,

There is wealth that mankind should pursue.

Section 2 : The relationship between money and the meaning of life.

"How to increase the wealth of all human beings?" Before I answer this question, I must first explain what money is. I must first explain: "The relationship between the meaning of life and money."

What is money? Why can this paper be used to buy things? Why can this paper be exchanged for goods and services? When I showed the banknote, the clerk allowed me to take his merchandise. When I showed the banknote, the clerk was willing to provide services for me. It was just a piece of paper. Why can the paper be exchanged for bread? Money is different from other papers. There is a seal of the king (government) on the money, which is based on the guarantee of the king (government), so the money is valuable.

Money is paper with credibility, the value of money comes from credibility, and the state is the support of money.

The state is the support of money. Money is very important, and the country is very important. If there is no country, no bank, no law, no police, your property will no longer be your property, your property will be taken away by robbers, and the people will not be able to live in peace.

"Money is very important, country is very important." Does mankind already know about this?

"Life is meaningful, people have an obligation to protect the environment, and people have an obligation to protect society." Does humanity already know about this?

The meaning of life is the most difficult topic in human history. Philosophers say: There is no answer to the meaning of life.

There is nothing humans have to do while they are alive.

Jesus and Buddha said: Money is not important, heaven is more important. Human beings are very contradictory. "The country is very important. We must protect our homeland, but life is meaningless, there is nothing humans have to do while they are alive.

The author discovered this contradiction.

The author discovered: "Life has meaning,

We must maintain our homeland. This is what we should live to do."

People cooperate with each other, and then there will be a country,There is also a dependency behind the country.

There are more law-abiding people than non-law-abiding people. There are more people who love peace than who love war. There are more normal people than crazy people. There are more people who have the will to survive than those who don't. When most people are willing to defend our lives, the country can exist. "Human beings are willing to survive, and people cooperate with each other, and then there will be a country and then there will be money."

Section 3 : Why do humans have to work?

First is survival, first is the will to survive, human beings cooperate with each other, then there is a country, and then there is money.

The title of this paper is: "How to increase the wealth of all human beings?"

Before I answer this question, I will explain in this section: "Why do humans have to work?"

The meaning of life is the most difficult topic in human history.

"What do people live to do ?" No philosopher can answer this question. And the author discovered: "Life is meaningful, and human beings have work that must be done."

How did the topic of the meaning of life come about?

Because there are humans on the earth and humans live on the earth, humans are forced to face today, and humans are forced to face "what are we going to do today? What are we going to do while we are alive?".

Then there is the topic of the meaning of life.

Money is the same, "Why do humans have to work?"

Because humans have bodies and because they are hungry, humans must work.

Life is meaningful, because humans have bodies and because they are hungry, humans must work.

Same,

Because humans own the earth, they must maintain the earth.

I have my home, I have to clean up my room,

I have my hometown, and my hometown needs someone to sweep the fallen leaves and clear water ditch.

I have a peaceful and lawful hometown, and I have to pay taxes to the police.

Because humans have bodies, they must exercise.

Because I have family members, I have to keep in touch.

Because I have today, so I must arrange today,

Because I have a mind, I must manage my mind, I need entertainment, and I need love.

"How to increase the wealth of all human beings?"

The answer to this question will not be as beautiful as the politicians brag about. The earth's resources are fixed. Humans are always hungry. Humans must always work for food. The society is running. We must always maintain the social mechanism. Even if I have a long vacation, I also need to arrange my vacation, even if I stay in the room. I also need to manage my mind.

Life is meaningful, because humans have bodies, earth, and minds, so humans must work.

Section 4 : How to increase the wealth of all human beings?

Because of hunger, humans must work.

Because humans must maintain social mechanisms, maintain the environment, and maintain their minds, humans must work.

Eat, digest, eat, digest, the Buddha said that food is nothingness after all.

Eat, digest, eat, digest,

There are many fruits in the author's hometown, and sometimes we discard fruits because of too many fruits. "How to increase the wealth of all human beings?" The answer is not more fruits and more factories. Because hunger is fixed, the answer is not: "Cut down the forest, plant more farmland, and build more factories."

How to increase the wealth of all human beings?

The answer is not to print more money. The answer is not to cut down the forest and plant more farmland.

How to increase the wealth of all human beings?

The topic is "The Meaning of Life",

What do people live to do ?

What must human beings pursue ?

What is the wealth of all mankind?

Eat, digest, eat, digest, meal after meal, meal after meal, after digestion, do humans get anything?

Can we leave anything to the future?

Yes, there is . Eating, digesting, eating, digesting, eating is not static, we are different from people a thousand years ago, we have ice cream, this is a great invention, this is our wealth.

A thousand years ago, humans often walked and walked around, and we often walked and walked around, but we have cars, which are our wealth. We have traffic lights, we have traffic rules, and traffic rules protect our safety. This is our wealth.

A thousand years ago, humans only knew that they wanted to catch more fish from the river, and we knew that we should protect our homeland. We have laws, we have cultivated ethics, and we have the concepts and habits of protecting the environment. This is our wealth.

In the past, farmers were oppressed by big landlords. No matter how hard they work, farmers will never become wealthy. Now in my hometown, workers can form unions, and workers can march on the streets. This is our wealth.

In the past, the people only knew to listen to the king. The king often took away the people's wealth like robbers. Now we know that we have an obligation to supervise the government. The concept of "We have an obligation to supervise the government" is our wealth.

In the past, mankind often wars. Now mankind knows that war is terrible. Mankind knows that nuclear weapons are terrible. The fear of war is our wealth. The concept of "We have an obligation to maintain peace" is our wealth.

In the past, human beings didn't know "what do people live to do ?".

Because of boredom and confusion, many people choose to seek excitement, many people choose to cause trouble, and many people choose to bully the weak.

The author has discovered that life is meaningful, and people have an obligation to maintain their own minds. The author's discovery is the wealth of all mankind. Now there are cartoons, there are many competitions, and there are many ways to laugh and sweat. This is the wealth of all mankind.

In the past, mankind was afraid of the end of the world, and mankind did not know to prepare for sustainability. In the past, there was no answer to the meaning of life, and humans were afraid to think about the meaning of life. Politicians are shouting patriotism and value, but no one has ever answered why we should be patriotic. The author found that life is meaningful: "Humans have an obligation to maintain the environment, and humans have an obligation to take responsibility for themselves."

There is a foundation of wealth. There are more people who love themselves than those who don't. There are more people who care about society than people who don't. There are more people who care about the environment than people who don't. There are more people who have the will to survive than people who don't.

This is the wealth of all mankind.

Everyone becomes rich. This is the progress of civilization, the progress of science that can be turned into words, and the increase of love and the will to survive that cannot be turned into words.

Section 5 : Comparison and Application.

The author found out: "First is survival, first the will to survive, then peace and cooperation, and then wealth."

The author discovered: "The world's resources are fixed, and human hunger is also fixed. How can we increase human wealth? The answer is enrichment of the mind and cultural progress."

This is a simple discovery, and is this a new discovery? And is this an important discovery? In this section, the author will explain what changes the author's findings will bring. This section is of comparison and application.

1. Desire.

"Limited resources, endless desires ."

In order to satisfy the infinite desires of mankind, you should learn to manage money, so you should study economics. This is a preface to economics.

"Because of desire, you should make money."

This is wrong. Desire is optional. Desire is not belief. Desire is not the driving force of human progress.

"Because of desire, you should make money."

Such a concept cannot answer: "How to increase human wealth?"

If desire is the driving force of wealth, when mankind wants to increase wealth, when man wants to increase driving force, man must increase desire and become more greedy?

And the author's answer is: according to the characteristics of nature,

Human beings have the obligation to maintain the environment, to maintain their own minds, and to strengthen their belief in survival. The belief in survival is the wealth of mankind.

2. Profit and Justice.

"In order to satisfy the infinite desires of mankind, you should learn to manage money." Desire is a negative word, and there are often conflicts between interest and justice.

Jesus said: It is difficult for rich people to enter the kingdom of heaven.

The Buddha said: Money is the dust that covers the soul.

The school teacher said: the pursuit of profit is the villain, the pursuit of morality is the gentleman.

Being rich is the dream of mankind, but there is no answer to the meaning of life. "Should people pursue wealth?" There is no answer. Human beings are not sure whether they should pursue wealth.

Humans are contradictory and helpless. "Humans are not sure if they should pursue wealth, but we are not saints. We have desires, so we pursue wealth."

People used to think like this.

In politics, people who support democracy and human rights have also made the same mistake. "Democratic values" and "universal values". People who support democracy are shouting democratic values, and the US government is shouting universal values.

Value is subjective, and people don't know whether democracy is subjective or objective. People who support democracy say: "Although democracy cannot be eaten, democracy is very important."

And the author found: "Science can be eaten, and democracy can be eaten."

"Democracy can be eaten. Democracy truly affects our lives. Isn't it a matter of course?" Some readers may misunderstand this. No, this is not taken for granted. In the past, democracy was doctrine and value. The US government shouted: universal value. In the past, people couldn't distinguish between subjectivity and objectivity. "Democracy is objective." This concept is the author's discovery.

3. The blueprint for the future.

"In order to satisfy desire, you should make money." Desire did not point out the blueprint for the future.

The meaning of life is a difficult problem, and mankind has no blueprint for the future. Where will the national budget be spent? How are we going to build our country? What future are we heading toward? There are no answers to these questions.

So people only know to build more factories and taller buildings.

And the author discovered: "What should human beings do in the next ten thousand years? The answer to this question is sustainability."

We must build a warm and sustainable home.

4. Science will bring destruction?

Is science good for mankind? Can science bring happiness? Will science bring destruction?

Humans have such doubts about science. When astronomy developed, the church persecuted scientists. When mankind was preparing to land on the moon, many people felt scared, worried that stepping on the moon would offend God. Humans are afraid of nature, and humans are also afraid of science.

In fear, science has progressed, but humans believe that life is meaningless and there is no future direction. Humans are stepping on messy steps, doing things that harm the environment, and doing things that harm each other. When humans taste the bitter fruit, humans say: Science will harm people, knowledge will harm people, and wealth will also harm people.

And the author found:

The earth's resources are roughly fixed. Day after day, meal after meal, can human beings accumulate any wealth?

Yes, mankind can know nature better, mankind can know mankind better, learn to get along with nature, learn to get along with each other, and enrich the mind.

Man's understanding of nature is human wealth.

5. Play and environmental protection.

In the old concept, the pursuit of morality is noble, the pursuit of interest is vulgar, and morality and interest conflict. Similarly, those who value environmental protection are noble, and those who value interests are vulgar. Environmental protection and interests conflict. Similarly, mind and matter often conflict, love and bread often conflict, play and serious reading often conflict.

Especially in Confucius' education, reading can contribute to society, and playing is a waste of life.

Regarding these conflicts, although some people say that we should balance.

But the conflict between interest and justice has not been resolved. The conflict between environmental protection and interest continues, and the conflict between play and serious reading continues.

And the author discovered:

"Maintaining the environment is not because of subjective values, and maintaining the mind is not because of subjective values. This is an objective fact. Human beings have the earth and human beings have the mind. Human beings have an obligation to maintain the earth and the mind. This is human work."

6. Government budget.

The author's hometown is Taiwan. Like other governments in the world, our government will formulate a big plan every few years, and then the congress will pass many budgets.

Politicians will build a lot of things. After building a lot of things, the politicians can show off: "Look! My political achievements are really rich."

It is the habit of politicians to fight for more budgets, build more things, pursue "greatness," and then show off.

But don't you pursue "greatness"? How will the government's budget be spent? What should we pursue if we do not pursue "greatness"?

In the next ten thousand years, what must mankind have to pursue?

Regarding the future, what must we pursue?

Life is the topic, life is the answer, and what human beings should pursue is "daily life."

Don't vanity projects, what the people want is infrastructure.

It's okay to build less projects. The country is not pursuing greatness.

The state pursues normality and health.

7. Competition.

Should humans compete with each other?

This is also a difficult problem.

Some people think that humans should compete. If people who work hard get the same amount of money as people who don't work hard, it is unfair. Competition helps mankind progress, so we should support capitalism.

Some people think that humans should not compete, and that everyone should eat the same bread. And now that science and technology have become more advanced, the rich have the help of machines, and those without machines and capital will definitely lose. Sweat cannot be exchanged for bread, and the poor will become poorer and poorer. So we should oppose capitalism.

In the past, there was no answer to the meaning of life. There was no answer to the question "How should humans live?" There was no answer to the question "Should humans compete?"

And the author found that life has meaning.

Human beings have an obligation to maintain their stomachs, and humans also have an obligation to maintain society.

Eating is the eternal pursuit of mankind, and peace is also the eternal pursuit of mankind.

When peace comes, humans still have to eat every day, and restaurants have to serve dishes every day, and there is a competition between delicious and unpalatable food.

Human beings have to eat every day, the competition in the restaurant will continue forever, and the competition among various professions will continue forever.

But this is competition, this is not war. When people are competing, the people also have an obligation to remind the country, people must ask the country to take care of the people who fall.

8. The assistance of the United Nations.

When the United Nations is helping backward countries,

The United Nations has also encountered similar problems:

"How to make the whole country rich?"

They will provide financial assistance and material assistance.

The United Nations knows: Teaching a man how to fish is better than giving him a fish.

The United Nations also provides educational assistance.

Build schools and teach students a skill. The United Nations also builds toilets and water purification equipment and solar power generation equipment...

Can this make a country rich?

There are other problems.

Advanced countries cannot help countries that refuse to work for themselves.

The dictators of backward countries are profligate, but the people are still indifferent. The people do not resist. The people don't care that their taxes are wasted. Most of the aid is taken away by the dictators. The country's wealth cannot be accumulated.

The people are indifferent and then the country is poor.

But how can we tell the people not to be indifferent?

The United States is trying to export democracy,

The United States said: Democracy is precious.

But the United States did not say: Life is meaningful and life is precious.

When faced with terrorism,

The United States is still saying different things.

Terrorists believe that the meaning of life is to sacrifice vigorously for God. The meaning of life is to avenge the unfairness of the world. The meaning of life is to carve deep pain.

But philosophers still say: The meaning of life is an unsolvable problem.

The United States said: Democracy is precious.

The United States did not say that life is meaningful and life is precious.

Section 6 : Conclusion.

Life is not nonentity, human beings live on the earth.

Mankind is forced to face today, mankind is forced to face hunger, mankind must satisfy hunger, mankind must fill today, mankind must satisfy the mind.

This is a forced blessing, Humans must pursue wealth.

Life is not nonentity, human beings live on the earth.

Mankind faces the earth, and mankind has the obligation to maintain the earth,

The earth is the only home for mankind.

How to increase the wealth of all human beings?

What wealth can we add to our homeland?

We can increase ethics, we can establish a legal system, we can establish the habit of protecting the environment, we can establish the habit of caring about society, we can develop science, and we can learn more about nature. Humans can always pursue the next meal, humans can always pursue peace, and humans can pursue music and laughter.

Life is meaningful. In the next ten thousand years, mankind should enrich the mind, and mankind should build a warm civilization.

Is tomorrow unknown? The meaning of life and the characteristics of tomorrow.

Section 1 : Preface.

At the graduation ceremony, the president of the university often tells graduates: "You are leaving the campus. You will face an unknown future and there will be unknown challenges. The teachers have no answers about the future. You have to find the answers by yourself."

This is an unsolved problem,

Tomorrow is unknown, and there is no answer to the future.

Like the meaning of life,

"What are you going to do tomorrow?"

"What are you going to do in the future?"

"What should people do in life?"

There is no answer to this question,

"Tomorrow" and "the meaning of life" are the most difficult topics.

Is tomorrow unknown?

This article will explain the questions and answers,

This article will first explain "people's fear and contradiction about tomorrow" and then explain the answer.

This paper will explain:

1. The old ideas and the shortcomings of the old ideas.

2. There are constant things.

3. The characteristics of tomorrow.

4. Comparison and application.

This paper will explain: Life has meaning and tomorrow has characteristics. There is a bright future, and that is the direction of mankind.

Section 2 : The old ideas and the shortcomings of the old ideas.

In the past concept: tomorrow is unknown.

Scientists believe that the future is unpredictable.

Jesus said: The judgment of the end will come suddenly.

The Buddha said: You may not be able to see the sun tomorrow.

Both science and religion say: tomorrow is unknown.

Maybe today is a normal day, I have breakfast with my family, and go to work or school after breakfast, but accidents may come suddenly at any time, and everything I love may suddenly disappear.

Tomorrow is unknown, which means that the beauty of today may disappear at any time. The idea of "tomorrow is unknown" affects today.

Are your efforts today correct? Is your effort today worth it? Work hard to do a good job in the company, hoping to let your family live a good life and accumulate good memories with your family. Is it right to work hard for this little happiness? Is this little happiness really valuable?

Not necessarily. Tomorrow is unknown. What is precious today may change tomorrow.

The Buddha said: Family love is short-lived.

Jesus said: Only the love of God is eternal.

In the face of an unknown future, the beauty of the present is as fragile as a bubble,

The efforts of ordinary people are useless.

Knowledge is the same. Human knowledge is cheap in God's eyes. Knowledge today may be wrong tomorrow. Ordinary people cannot touch the truth.

Because tomorrow is unknown, you cannot be sure that your knowledge today is correct.

Because tomorrow is unknown, you cannot be sure that what you have done today is worth it.

Because tomorrow is unknown, the good and evil of today are uncertain.

Because tomorrow is unknown, everything today is uncertain, and people do not have a certain knowledge.

The concept that "tomorrow is unknown" brings uncertainty.

This concept also brings fear.

The question "Tomorrow is unknown"

brings up another question: "Love will disappear, right?"

Love is not forever!

There is no eternal love!

Oaths are often false.

The person I hold tightly today, as time goes on, the warmth in my arms is very fragile, and the warmth in my arms will soon disappear.

Wealth is not eternal, food is always digested in a short time, even health and tangible everything is as fragile.

Is "love" really worthy of being loved?

Can "love" stand the test of time?

Is "love" right?

Maybe we should not value the love of ordinary people,

Maybe we should seek the eternal love of God.

Tomorrow is uncertain,

Love is also uncertain,

Therefore, human beings often feel doubts and fears.

"Unknown" brings negative effects.

The concept that "tomorrow is unknown" brings uncertainty,

This concept also brings confusion.

The question "Tomorrow is unknown" brings up another question: "Life is meaningless."

Tomorrow is unknown, and things that are valuable today may become worthless tomorrow.

There is no real value in the world, and mankind cannot leave wealth for tomorrow.

What should human beings pursue in life? The philosopher's answer is "I don't know."

Should I pursue profit?

But money cannot buy tickets to the kingdom of heaven. Money is not eternal. Fame, status, and wealth are fragile. Accidents and death will come at any time.

People are bound to die.

Money is not equal to happiness. Even if you hold happiness, happiness will soon be lost from your hands over time.

It's meaningless to pursue profit.

Shouldn't I pursue profit?

Should I pursue unprofitable happiness?

Pile dominoes, play games, read comics, play chess, draw, sing, set off fireworks...

In the same way, unprofitable happiness is not eternal, happiness is just happiness, happy times always pass quickly, and nothing is left after the fireworks disappear.

Whatever people do is meaningless.

Because "tomorrow is unknown",

So "what should human beings do for tomorrow?

What should we leave for tomorrow? "

There is no answer to this question.

Because "tomorrow is unknown",

So "what kind of future should mankind head toward? "

There is no answer to this question.

So human beings live in a daze,

pursuing profit for a while, and then pursuing unprofitable happiness for a while.

But people said : "The pursuit of profit is meaningless."

But people said: "The pursuit of unprofitable happiness is meaningless."

Tomorrow is unknown, "What should humans live to do?" There is no answer to the question, people have no future direction, and people live in a daze.

Section 3 : There are constant things.

Tomorrow is a difficult question,

"What should humans live to do?"

is a difficult question,

The meaning of life is the most difficult subject in human history.

Humans don't know what to do in life,

People have always been afraid of tomorrow.

And in this section, the author will explain: "Tomorrow has characteristics, and there are constant things."

Tomorrow is unknown, mankind has not found eternity, mankind has not found something that will not change in the future.

This is an old concept.

Are there constant things in nature?

Yes, humans have found it,

But humans don't know: "It has been found."

People still can't overcome fear,

People are still confused.

This is a contradictory and confusing thing.

Tomorrow is unknown.

A law of physics that has been tested 10,000 times.

Tomorrow, if I do the ten thousand and one, will I get the same result?

I don't know, because I haven't done it yet, and the result is uncertain. This is the limit of science and scientists cannot predict the future.

A law of physics that has been tested 10,000 times.

Tomorrow, if I do the ten thousand and one, will I get the same result?

Know and be sure that if the conditions remain the same, the results will definitely be the same, and the laws of physics will not change.

Have scientists discovered anything that will not change?

Yes, science is to understand nature, and then find the laws from it. Nature has laws, and scientists have discovered many reproducible laws.

The earth revolves around the sun, nature has regularity,

Picking up things and letting them go, Newton discovered: "The earth has the power to attract objects." This is a characteristic of nature that can be reproduced over and over again.

Archimedes discovered the principle of buoyancy two thousand years ago. You can also take a bath or experiment. The principle of buoyancy is a characteristic of nature that can be reproduced again and again.

Have humans discovered things that will not change?

It seems to be and it doesn't seem to be.

Humans don't know: "It has been found."

Mankind cannot overcome the fear of tomorrow.

And the author discovered this contradiction in human beings,

The author discovered that "Tomorrow has characteristics",

"Tomorrow has certain characteristics,

Life is definitely meaningful. "This is the author's discovery.

Section 4 : The characteristics of tomorrow.

What are the characteristics of tomorrow?

Is there anything that is still right after ten thousand years?

Yes, the sun has a lifespan of several billion years. Ten thousand years later, the sun will still be there.

The earth has existed for billions of years,

before the demise of mankind,

the earth will always be there.

If we prepare a control group that maintains the environment and an experimental group that does not maintain the environment, we will find that people have an obligation to maintain the environment. "People have an obligation to maintain the environment." This is still right after 10,000 years.

If we prepare sober volunteers and drunk volunteers, and then let them play racing games, or change to other situations in life, we will find that people must pay attention to their own safety. "People have an obligation to take care of themselves."

This is still right after 10,000 years.

If human beings stop maintaining social functions, social functions will cease. "People are obliged to maintain society." This is still right after 10,000 years.

If mankind stops maintaining peace, mankind will lose peace. "Humanity has an obligation to maintain peace."

This is still right after 10,000 years.

"All living things metabolize, and humans have the need to eat. If humans survive, they need to eat."

This is still right after 10,000 years.

"Humans have the ability to think, humans have minds, and humans have emotional needs. If humans survive, humans must take care of their minds, humans must love, and humans must always love."

This is still right after 10,000 years.

These are the characteristics of tomorrow,

These are the answers to "What should human live to do ?"

Section 5 : Comparison and Application.

The author found out: "The sun is always there, and tomorrow we have to eat well."

The author discovered: "Life is meaningful, and there is something to be done tomorrow."

This is a simple discovery, and is this a new discovery? And is this an important discovery? In this section, the author will explain what changes the author's findings will bring. This section is of comparison and application.

1. When a teenager asks: "What is the meaning of life?".

In the past philosophers answered :   "I don't know ".

In the future, school teachers should no longer answer that they don't know. The school should tell students that life really has meaning.

2. In the past, humans lived in fear. Humans were afraid of the night, lightning, nature, and tomorrow. And the author found out: "The sun is always there, and tomorrow we have to eat well." Tomorrow has a clear direction, and for the next 10,000 years, humans should continue to protect the earth.

3. Human beings have an obligation to maintain society and the environment, and human beings have an obligation to be responsible for themselves. Schools should tell students: "You have an obligation." Schools should not say: "I don't know, I'm not sure."

4. Tomorrow is unknown. Human knowledge is always a little uncertain. Religiousists always say: "In the eyes of God, human beings know nothing." And the author found something certain: "The next ten thousand years, mankind must continue to love the earth." Without relying on God, the author discovered something certain.

5. Love will disappear. The Buddha said that eating is not important. The Buddha said that family love is as fragile as a bubble. Jesus said that only God's love is eternal. Buddha was wrong,

Buddha only saw

Food will digest and disappear. The Buddha didn't know: "As long as people are still alive, people have to eat all the time."

The Buddha didn't know: "As long as human beings are still alive on earth, human beings must always love."

6. Which is better, democracy or dictatorship?

There has been no answer to this question.

Man is not the God. Who can say that he is right about the future?

Kings and elites are not necessarily right, but the majority are not necessarily right.

Because the future is unknown, right and wrong are uncertain, and whether democracy or dictatorship is better is uncertain.

And the author found: "Life is meaningful, and people have an obligation to care about society."

Autocratic countries do not allow people to care about society, so the dictatorship is wrong.

The author's discovery is true and certain,

Democracy and dictatorship are no longer endless disputes.

7. Tomorrow is unknown, and human knowledge is always a little uncertain.

And the author found: "Tomorrow has characteristics, and there are certain things."

After having a certain foundation, people can accumulate on this foundation.

There are many repeatability things in nature, and humans can describe nature's characteristics in more detail.

With a certain foundation, humans can accumulate more certain wisdom.

Section 6 : Conclusion.

The author found out: "There are characteristics of tomorrow."

The author found out: "

There are the characteristics of nature,

There are the characteristics of life,

Human beings have an obligation to maintain the environment, an obligation to care about society, an obligation to think, and an obligation to take responsibility for themselves. "

The author's discovery is a simple discovery, but it is an important discovery.

Maybe some readers will misunderstand, maybe some readers will think that this is something that humans have known for a long time. The author emphasizes once again that the meaning of life is the most difficult topic in human history. All philosophers who challenged this topic have failed. Mankind lives in doubt and fear. Humans are worried about the end of the world that will come at any time. Humans sing love but are not sure whether love is really worthy of being loved.

"There are characteristics of tomorrow, and life has meaning."

This is the author's discovery.

Transitional Justice and the Meaning of Life

Section 1 : Preface.

The author's hometown is Taiwan, which used to be authoritarian.

Taiwan is now on the road of democracy. The people of Taiwan can vote for the president, and the people of Taiwan have the freedom of belief. When we are introducing democracy, we will talk about freedom of belief.

This is a contradiction. Once, people who believe in democracy and those who believe in authoritarianism had a fierce conflict.

When we are introducing democracy, we should not say: "Faith is free." We should explain the history of the conflict, we should explain: "Why can't we believe in authority?"

Transitional justice means that "justice" has changed,

Culture and beliefs changed,

"How should we live?" There is a new answer to this question.

This paper will explain:

1. The relationship between justice and the meaning of life.

2. Authoritarianism is the justice of the past.

3. Freedom and try to find new answers.

4. New answers.

Transitional justice is the change of justice,

This paper will explain "How should we live?"

This paper will explain:

Why was the old age wrong?

What is the new answer? "

Section 2 : The relationship between justice and the meaning of life.

Mankind appeared on the earth, so mankind was forced to face "today", mankind was forced to face the question of "how should one live?" This is the origin of the topic of the meaning of life, and philosophers gave it the answer : I don't know.

Similarly, you are not the only person on the earth. There are many people on the earth. Human beings have to face other people. The question "How should one live?" becomes "How should we live?" and this is "justice" .

"How should we live?"

Is there a common answer?

Does universal value exist?

What's right? what is wrong?

What is kindness? What is evil?

Is there any rule,

Which rule should everyone follow?

What accords with that law is justice,

Whatever violates that law is an error.

Is there any direction,

Which direction is our country pursuing?

What fits that direction is justice,

Whatever violates that direction is an error.

"Does justice exist?"

that is

"Does a common law exist?"

Are there any laws that all humans should obey?

Section 3 : The core issue of transitional justice.

Taiwan lies to the southeast of China. After World War II, Chiang Kai-shek was defeated by the Communist Party.

Chiang Kai-shek brought two million people from China to Taiwan. Chiang Kai-shek exercised authoritarian rule in Taiwan.

The supporters of Chiang Kai-shek believed that: Chiang Kai-shek was a hero of World War II. Chiang Kai-shek led the country through difficult times. Chiang Kai-shek's supporters erected many bronze statues for Chiang Kai-shek.

Under the bronze statue read: "National Hero."

Chiang Kai-shek is a hero of justice, and Chiang Kai-shek is the justice of Taiwan.

People fighting for freedom believe that Chiang Kai-shek is a dictator who exercises authoritarian rule. Under the dictatorship, Chiang Kai-shek has killed many Taiwanese and Chiang Kai-shek is a murderer.

Those fighting for freedom said: "Authority is not good, dictators are evil, Chiang Kai-shek is evil, and the bronze statue is a symbol of authority."

But why?

Why is authority wrong?

Why is democracy right?

Because people who support freedom have gained power,

So democracy is right?

People who support freedom have never given an explanation.

Why is Chiang Kai-shek evil?

Are you the God ? Why do you judge people?

Chiang Kai-shek was a hero of World War II before,

Why is he considered a big villain now?

What is the basis of the trial?

"The old age is evil, and the new age is justice, right? Why?"

This is the first problem in transitional justice.

The ruling party in Taiwan is now dismantling the bronze statue,

The place where the bronze statue of Chiang Kai-shek was

originally placed,

What are you going to put now?

What is the new justice? (What is the value of Taiwan?)

This is the second problem in transitional justice.

"Why was the old age wrong?" and "What is the new idea?"

These are the two major issues in transitional justice.

Many people who support freedom did not think about this issue.

Instead, they directly believe that bronze statues are a symbol of authority and that bronze statues are all evil.

"Why was the old age wrong?" and "What is the new idea?"

These are the core issues of transitional justice.

Section 4 : Authoritarianism is the old justice.

Why was the old age wrong? Before the author answers this question,

The author will first explain what is the answer of the old age.

There was a big earthquake in Taiwan, and Taiwanese set up a monument in the disaster area.

The monument reminds the next generation: Don't forget the power of nature.

This is the essence of bronze statues. Like monuments, bronze statues are exhortations.

"What is the most important thing in life?"

"How should people live?"

The bronze statue is the answer to this question.

There are too many books in the library,

If we can only tell the next generation one sentence,

What are we going to keep? The bronze statue represents that sentence,

The bronze statue is the summary of culture. The bronze statue is the answer to the meaning of life.

A huge statue of Christ was erected in Rio, Brazil,

This means that Brazil is telling the next generation:

"How should people live? People have to listen to God's words,

What is the most important thing in life? The most important thing in life is to listen to God's words,

The meaning of life is God. "

The disciples of Confucius erected a bronze statue of Confucius, which means:

"How should people live? The king behaves like a king. The courtier behaves like a courtier. The father behaves like a father. The son behaves like a son.

and the meaning of life is courtesy. "

Some people have erected bronze statues of aboriginal heroes, which means:

"Don't forget to resist, don't forget the ancestral spirit."

Some people have erected bronze statues of rescue heroes, which means:

"The meaning of life is to sacrifice oneself to save others."

Some people have erected bronze statues of legendary athletes, which means:

"The meaning of life is never to give up."

And the bronze statue of the national leader represents:

"The meaning of life is loyalty."

Loyalty is the good of the old age.

Disloyalty is evil.

Section 5 : The Shortcomings of Loyalty.

What is good? How should people live?

What should we obey?

The answer in the past was "loyalty."

People in the past didn't know what was good,

When there is conflict in society, who should listen to whom?

Intuitively and without reason, children should listen to their parents, and the people should listen to the king. Because the king is a king, we should listen to the king. Because the king is the king, then there is law and order, and then the country can be maintained, and the people can be protected by law. If the generals lose their loyalty, it will be a series of wars.

"Based on the will of God and the king, people should abide by the law." The concept of loyalty is the foundation of the law. Loyalty is good, and loyalty is the answer to "How should people live?"

But "the king is equal to the law" is dangerous, because while the king is maintaining order, the king is the most indulgent person, and even the king is a blood-stained person.

Chiang Kai-shek is similar,

Supporters of Chiang Kai-shek believed that Chiang Kai-shek protected and stabilized the country, but Chiang Kai-shek's hands were stained with blood.

Section 6 : Freedom and the shortcomings of freedom.

"The king equals the law" is dangerous. So some people stood up against the king, and at the same time challenged old ideas. People should not be loyal, people should be free, the future of the country should not be determined by the king, and the future of the country should be determined by the majority. Power should not be centralized, and power should be dispersed.

"What is good?" There is no standard answer to this question.

Those who support freedom have not answered what good is, and the reason for freedom is just resistance.

Those who advocate freedom say: "I advocate freedom."

Those who advocate loyalty say: "I advocate loyalty."

You have your opinion, I have my opinion,

The two sides quarreled.

Those who support freedom say: "Freedom is the universal value."

Those who support loyalty say: "Loyalty is the universal value."

People who support freedom say: "Freedom is wonderful."

Those who support loyalty say: "Freedom can be chaotic."

Those who support freedom say: "The future of the country should be determined by the people."

The supporter of loyalty said, "Are the majority right? We are ordinary people. It is better to listen to the king."

Those who support freedom say: "The dictator's hands are stained with blood."

Those who support loyalty say: "The king has merits and demerits. Don't jump to conclusions. On what basis do you judge people, are you the God? Supporting loyalty is my freedom. Why do you control me?"

People who support loyalty say: "Loyalty is good."

Those who support freedom say: "There is no standard answer."

There is no standard answer to good, why should those who support loyalty listen to those who support freedom? So transitional justice fell into a long quarrel.

Section 7 : Search for new value.

Freedom is anti-authority. People who support freedom think that freedom is a new value, but they also feel puzzled. Freedom is just anti-authority. We don't have new value yet. Taiwan needs new value.

Taiwan is demolishing Chiang Kai-shek's bronze statue,

The place where the bronze statue of Chiang Kai-shek was originally placed,

What are you going to put now?

What is the new value? What is the value of Taiwan? So Taiwanese strive to find new value.

There is a sacred mountain in Taiwan, and that sacred mountain has prevented Taiwan from typhoon disasters. The sacred mountain is strong and great, and the value of Taiwan is the spirit of the sacred mountain.

Taiwanese people are generally enthusiastic, and Taiwan value is enthusiasm.

The ancestors of Taiwanese have a deep relationship with the cow. The cow worked hard to cultivate the fields. The cow is not afraid of hardship. The value of Taiwan is the cow spirit.

There is a female vegetable vendor in Taiwan. Her education is not high. She has continued to donate money in silence for decades and continue to help disadvantaged groups. This is Taiwan's value.

There is a baseball pitcher in Taiwan. He was once the ace pitcher of the Yankees. Doing my job well, pitch by pitch, This is the value of Taiwan.

There is a hero in Taiwan who resists colonial rule. This is Taiwan's value.

There is a martyr in Taiwan,

He set himself on fire in order to fight for freedom. This is Taiwan's value.

There is a goddess who protects fishermen in Taiwan's beliefs. This is Taiwan's value.

China is very hateful. To resist China's threat, It is Taiwan's value.

President Tsai Ing-wen of Taiwan said: "Taiwan consensus is to build consensus through democratic procedures."

The value of Taiwan is that we have to find the value of Taiwan,

You say a great thing, I say a great thing,

Everyone says a great thing, and then we discuss it together, then we can find the value of Taiwan!

You say a great thing, I say a great thing,

Taiwanese find the value of Taiwan in the same way as humans find the meaning of life.

Some people say that the meaning of life is to serve society,

Some people say that the meaning of life is sacrifice,

Some people say that the meaning of life is humor,

Some people say that the meaning of life is music,

Some people say that the meaning of life is to protect family members,

Some people say that the meaning of life is to find peace in the heart,

Some people say that the meaning of life is to play like a puppy,

Some people say that the meaning of life is to challenge the limit,

Some people say that the meaning of life is to learn to endure hardship,

Some people say that the meaning of life is reading,

Some people say that the meaning of life is to go back to heaven,

Some people say that the meaning of life is to get ahead,

Some people say that the meaning of life is to make close friends,

Some people say that the meaning of life is to taste good coffee......

There are many answers, but why is that answer?

The reason? really?

There are many answers to the value of Taiwan and the meaning of life.

But each answer is unreasonable.

Section 8 : The author's answer.

Does life have meaning? What should people live to do ? Are there any laws that all mankind should abide by?

The meaning of life used to be the most difficult question in human history, and I have found the answer.

The author found that nature has laws. Based on the laws of nature, life has meaning. The meaning of life is "self-decision ,diversity, to prosper together, sustain."

What should humans live to do? What should humans live to do in the next ten thousand years? Thinking about the next ten thousand years, the answer is "sustain." This is an answer that can be proved by experiments. As long as we prepare the experimental group that maintains the environment and the control group that does not maintain the environment, we can find that nature has laws, and we can find that humans are obliged to maintain the environment. This is what humans should do when they are alive. , The meaning of life is "sustain."

What should humans live to do? What should I do in my life? This is one thing to do. I must to answer my life. The answer is "self-decision." This is an answer that can be proved by experiments. As long as sober volunteers and drunken volunteers play racing games, it can prove the danger of being drunk, and it can also prove that people should pay attention to their own safety. Nature has such a law: people have the obligation to take care of themselves, people are responsible for their own life. The meaning of life is "self-decision ."

What should humans live to do? What are we going to do today?

We are responsible for "our today", and the answer is " to prosper together". This is an answer that can be proved by experiments. As long as someone cuts off water and electricity, it can prove that we are obliged to maintain social mechanisms.

Nature has such a law: We have an obligation to protect society. The meaning of life is " to prosper together".

What should people live to do? What am I going to do today?

The sun is there, "today" is there.

This is true, there is a blank today waiting for me to fill in, free play represents creativity, I must answer today, I must enrich my mind.

This is true, the blank today is right in front of us. The meaning of life is "diversity".

According to the laws of nature, everyone has an obligation to think, and the answer is "diversity."This is a rule that everyone should abide by.

Are people different from person to person?

People have similarities with people,

Everyone should take care of the environment,

Everyone should protect society,

Everyone should care about the country,

Everyone should be responsible for themselves.

There are similarities and differences between people.

This is also a same point,

Everyone should learn to respect.

According to the characteristics of nature,

The meaning of life is "self-decision ,diversity, to prosper together, sustain."

The author has discovered: Nature has laws.

The author found a common rule,

"How should we live?" There is a common answer to this question.

Why is dictatorship wrong? Because people have an obligation to care about society,

The dictatorship prohibits people from caring about the country. So dictatorship is wrong.

"Why was the old age wrong?" and "What is the new idea?"

The author has already answered these two questions.

Section 9 : The reaction of Taiwanese.

There is a contradiction that often appears in transitional justice,

Those who support freedom say: Freedom is human nature. Taiwanese love freedom. Taiwanese have been pursuing freedom a long time ago. Taiwanese have always loved freedom.

This is a contradiction: "The past was a dark age, but Taiwanese people have always loved freedom."

"Freedom is welcome, but the martyrs have been persecuted." People who support freedom often describe freedom as a fairy tale when they praise freedom.

The true transitional justice should be: "The old age was dark, people didn't like freedom, and people liked loyalty.

Those who we now consider to be martyrs, they used to be insurgents in the eyes of the public. "

Transitional justice is a process from not understanding to understanding,

New ideas are not popular at the beginning.

New ideas are not popular at the beginning,

The author found the answer:

"According to the laws of nature, people have an obligation to think, be responsible for themselves, have an obligation to care about society, and have an obligation to maintain the environment."

The meaning of life is "self-decision ,diversity, to prosper together, sustain." This is the future direction of Taiwan.

And when the author told the Taiwanese my answer,

Taiwanese are not happy,

The author got a little encouragement and a lot of ridicule.

"Wow! A madman said that he has found the answer to the meaning of life."

"I'm dying laughing. Let me tell you: there is no answer to the meaning of life."

Taiwan laughed at the author's answer,

Then a lot of "originally" appeared in Taiwan.

People originally should think,

People originally should not be indifferent,

People originally should be responsible for themselves,

The people have an obligation to supervise the country originally,

Taiwan is a community with a shared future originally,

Democracy is practical originally.

A strange "diversity" has appeared in Taiwan,

Because there is no answer to the meaning of life, Taiwan value is diversity.

Because Taiwan has mountains, seas, forests, and grasslands and Taiwan is rich in species, Taiwan value is diversity.

Because Taiwan has aboriginals, Chinese, and people from the Philippines, Vietnam, and Indonesia, Taiwan value is diversity.

Because of the advanced technology and the vigorous development of Taiwan, Taiwan value is diversity.

Because Taiwan has learned Chinese culture, Japanese culture, European culture, and its own local culture, Taiwan value is diversity.

Because God created a colorful world, Jesus supports diversity, and because Jesus supports diversity, Taiwan value is diversity.

Because the Buddha has no prejudices, we must learn to respect, so Taiwan value is diversity.

Because Taiwanese are enthusiastic and tolerant, Taiwan value is diversity.

"I'm dying laughing. Let me tell you: there is no answer to the meaning of life."

But the value of Taiwan suddenly has an answer.

President Tsai Ing-wen said: Taiwan value is "to prosper together".

Then the ministers, mayors, media, and scholars under President Tsai said that "to prosper together" is the best answer.

Then a lot of strange "to prosper together" appeared.

A politician said: Since I entered politics, I have always worked for the welfare of the masses. "to prosper together" has always been my political philosophy, and Taiwan value is "to prosper together".

Because "to prosper together" has always been the long-time wish of the Taiwanese, Taiwan value is "to prosper together".

Because Taiwan is our mother, Taiwan value is "to prosper together".

Because the martyrs sacrificed and resisted, and because the martyrs were brave and not selfish, Taiwan value is "to prosper together".

Because human rights are universal values, Taiwan value is "to prosper together".

Because Taiwanese are warm and hospitable, Taiwan value is "to prosper together".

Because we should love Taiwan, Taiwan value is "to prosper together".

How did the new answer come from?

No reason, no source, but there is an answer.

This is a strange thing.

Section 10 : Conclusion.

Transitional justice is "justice" and "process",

Transitional justice is

The process of people finding answers,

The process by which people accept answers.

Does justice exist?

Are there any common rules?

"Why was the old age wrong?

What is the new answer?"

Is there a process to explore the answer?

Is there a process for receiving answers?

Transitional justice means deep cultivation of culture, and the complete process from unknown to understanding is transitional justice.

In the past, justice was loyalty. Later, people fought for freedom. Because loyalty was not good, people looked for new answers.

In the past, life was meaningless, and people had nothing to do.

And now there is a new answer,

The author has discovered that life is meaningful, everyone should think, and everyone should care about society.

This paper answers:

"Why was the old age wrong?

What is the new answer?"

The author has found a common rule,

"How should we live?"

There is a common answer to this question.

怎麼增加人類全體的財富？
生命的意義與留給明天的財富。

How to increase the wealth of all human beings?
The meaning of life and the wealth left to tomorrow.

（中英雙語版）

作　　　者／決長（Jue Chang）
出版者／美商 EHGBooks 微出版公司
發行者／美商漢世紀數位文化公司
臺灣學人出版網：http：／／www.TaiwanFellowship.org
地　　　址／106 臺北市大安區敦化南路 2 段 1 號 4 樓
電　　　話／02-2701-6088 轉 616-617
印　　　刷／漢世紀古騰堡®數位出版 POD 雲端科技
出版日期／2022 年 2 月
總經銷／Amazon.com
臺灣銷售網／三民網路書店：http：／／www.sanmin.com.tw
　　　　三民書局復北店
　　　　　地址／104 臺北市復興北路 386 號
　　　　　電話／02-2500-6600
　　　　三民書局重南店
　　　　　地址／100 臺北市重慶南路一段 61 號
　　　　　電話／02-2361-7511
全省金石網路書店：http：／／www.kingstone.com.tw
定　　　價／新臺幣 450 元（美金 15 元 ／ 人民幣 100 元）

2022 年版權美國登記，未經授權不許翻印全文或部分及翻譯為其他語言或文字。
2022 © United States, Permission required for reproduction, or translation in whole or part.

www.ingramcontent.com/pod-product-compliance
Lightning Source LLC
LaVergne TN
LVHW091934070526
838200LV00068B/987